1460 Days

Drea Matsuda

BookLeaf
Publishing

India | USA | UK

1460 Days © 2024 Drea Matsuda

All rights reserved.

No part of this publication may be reproduced, stored in a retrieval system, or transmitted, in any form or by any means, electronic, mechanical, photocopying, recording or otherwise, without the prior written permission of the presenters.

Drea Matsuda asserts the moral right to be identified as the author of this work.

Presentation by *BookLeaf Publishing*

Web: www.bookleafpub.com

E-mail: info@bookleafpub.com

ISBN: 9789360940010

First edition 2024

Between you and me, I thought it would last a little while longer. But I'm learning to let go of what could have been.

ACKNOWLEDGEMENT

I want to say thank you to all the poets and writers that shared their words of wisdom and for inspiring me since I was a young girl. The power of the written word is astounding. It truly can heal and transform our lives.

To my family and friends: your love and support have sustained me through the highs and lows. Thank you for being patient when I went dark, when I wasn't present, and when I could barely recognize myself. Thank you for continuing to reach out when I didn't want to be reached - I didn't realize how much I needed it.

To you, dear reader: I hope what you read resonates with you, and you find comfort in knowing you are not the only one who has gone through despair, loss and betrayal.

And lastly, to love itself -- for its beauty, its pain and its endless capacity to surprise and teach.

PREFACE

In the labyrinth of the heart, there exists a delicate balance between passion and pain, desire and destruction. What you are about to read is not merely a gentle caress but a tempestuous storm about facing the truth.

There are moments of beauty and profound sorrow, where the boundaries of ecstasy and agony blur and fade. When experiencing these polarities, it's easy to get lost in the lies we tell ourselves and the ones our lovers tell us.

This is not for the faint of heart. Within these lines are hidden secrets, unspoken for over 1,460 days. However, solitude brings reflection and through the cathartic power of poetry we can emerge from the shadows; hopefully our hearts a little lighter, our souls a little wiser.

I hope you know that you are not alone in this journey. Unraveling the intricacies and darkness of love, loss, and revenge there is redemption, growth and forgiveness. It's through our shared experiences that we find our truest selves and discover resilience.

Silk

Like untying
a silk ribbon,
easily
you uncurled
my heart --
and instead of running
from
the darkness
you ran straight
into the abyss...
and showered me
with kisses

What is it
between
us two
that when our touch
combines
it's so electric
I feel ALIVE
and even one
hundred kisses
is never
enough

You make me
vulnerable --
defenses are down,
I'm powerless now,
unsure of how
to escape...
it would have
been easier
if we never got
back in touch
and I could keep
pretending
that my life was enough

We've been denying
whatever this is
and yet,
one hint
one look
from you
is all it took....

Addicted

check for texts
all day long --
like a drug,
i crave you
enable you

addicted
to your fingers
up and down my skin,
and your lips
your body
upon mine...

clean the mess we left behind
wipe mascara
running from

my eyes...
and your smile
gets me every time

this isn't right,
it's just so wrong --
and the truth is
i'm not fine
i'm not fine
i'm not fine

Reckless

always your gaze
set
my heart ablaze
it's hard
to look you
in the eye

in my heart i knew
through and through
i've wanted you
against my
common sense,
this longing
is reckless...

and now,
more than ever before,
tragedy stands between us -
how could this be real
if we aren't free to love?

years ago
i accepted
my fate
and now it's too late

to stop this

your touch
your words
make my soul ache....
my heart hurts
when
you're not around

i want to push you away...
but the more i do,
the pain remains

somehow we are meant to be
connected
intertwined --
yet still,
you're
not even
mine....

Behind

you embraced me
from behind
your body claiming mine,
no hesitation
or fear
(i've always belonged
to you, it's clear)

started by
kissing my neck
gently down to
where my shoulder bends
your hands
massaging my peaks...
every second passing slowly
sensually

as i get
weak
i trembled under your lips
as you hardened
behind my hips
(i want you so bad...)

your fingers
already
discovered me
wet with
anticipation
i closed my eyes
and waited --
you moaned with appreciation
'spread your legs now baby'

pushing the edges
of my panties aside
holding me tight
as you slide it inside
(omg..........)

you held me up
and went so deep
i could barely feel
my feet
faster and faster
'you're mine, you're mine,' you said

one hand wrapped around my neck --
i moaned helplessly
again and again
nectar trickling
down
as i collapsed
against the bed

Weak

There is no
choice
your voice
makes me
weak

i obey
when you're near
and that's
why i fear
you the
most

Changed

I can't be the person
you want me
to be
these years
have
changed
me

I'll only
break you
and
make you
cry
because I can't
forgive
what you've done
to me

I'm cold
as
ice

deep inside
the fire
has died

replaced by glass
and stone -

to be safe is to
be unloved
or alone.

Emptiness

Sometimes
I catch myself
feeling
so empty
that I wonder if
I'm even breathing

Hours...

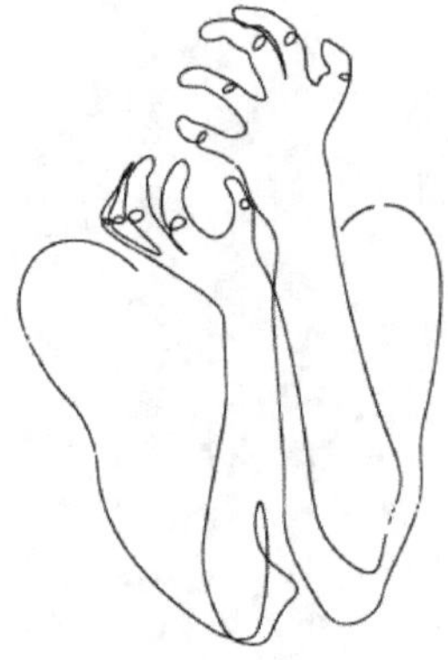

Hours ago
I had your heart
and a future
with you

Today
I'm alone
sickened and blue

Because now
you have to do
what you have to do --
stand by her side
as she lives the life
I was supposed to
live

with you

It's a pain
so
new to me
but I have to accept
it wasn't meant to be

Distance

you love
from a
distance
because our situation
forbids
us
being together

Edges

The edges of my broken heart
softened in your arms
and the shelter of
your presence
kept me from harm

And maybe that's why
this is so hard
why I feel
alone
because walking
away from you
is like leaving
home

Doesn't Matter

It doesn't matter what
I do or say
Someone's heart is breaking
either way

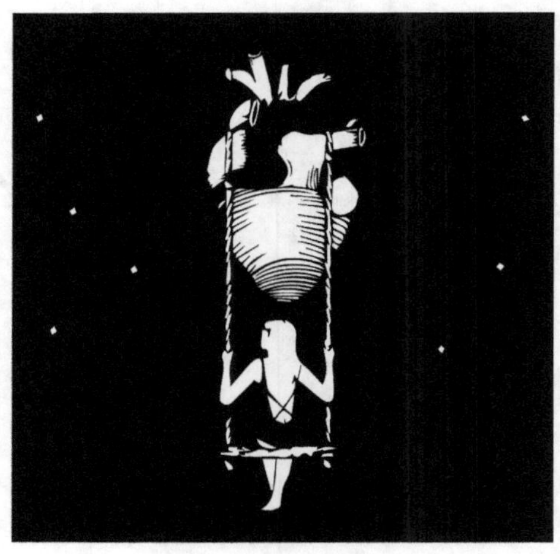

The Only Difference

we could
have
had an amazing
life
it was all so clear
but the wounds are
deep
blood still
seeps
like
yesterday

For you, it's easy
"Just let go, let the past go"
But you had a child
without
me --
while
we lost two of
our own...

He took the pain
away
when you
betrayed

me
I cried 1000 times...
you asked
if I still
love him
....I lied.

He wants me
to start
a life with him
I want to say yes --
you have no idea
I've been
keeping this
secret....

I thought my
love
was strong
enough
to get
through this...
but it turns out
I'm just as
screwed
up
as you...
the only difference
is

my love for you
was once
true...

If

If we were both
honest
how honest would we be
Let's face it babe
you've been silent
since the beginning
You told me things
but not everything

And now the road is
winding toward
the end
I've never loved
like this before
and I won't ever again

but you said let's
keep our love open,
I can't just be your friend...

If only we could have
done things
a little differently
we were ready
but never really
just two lost souls
that kept each other warm
during the storm

Again

I've been withering away since you left
mascara down my cheeks
muscles gone weak

the feeling of being in your arms
is where I truly belong
so why am I
the one to run
away now

you changed your mind
came back to town
you've given me the
run around
too many times for me to

believe what's true

and I've been withering away
since you said you wanted me
then changed your mind again
it's harder now
before back then...

what I wouldn't give
for another week with you
make me strong
make me whole again
my dearest lover
my sweetest friend...

I've been withering away
my bones are brittle
my skin is thin
need your warmth
to heat
this icy
heart again...

No One Knows

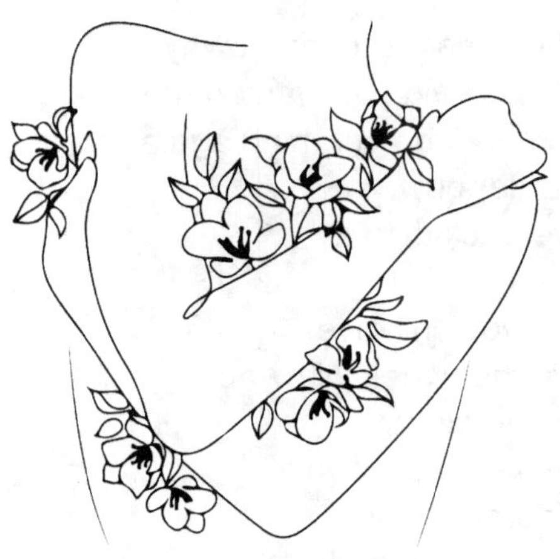

She walks
head down
when no one's
around,
sometimes you'll
catch a frown,
but rarely

She smiles so much
and laughs so loud
you'd never know
the feelings
she doesn't show

In the bathroom
and

shower she cries
every day
she lies
it will be okay,
just another day
another year
or two

But no one knows
what she's going through
or the thoughts
that fill her head
the ones that look
the happiest
are the ones said
to be
the darkest
inside

She's trying to escape
with all her might
pretending she's ok
the harder she tries
the more she lies
and the more she lies
the more she cries

And it never ends..

will it ever end?
The ache in her chest
won't seem to mend
but she can still
play pretend
and smile
and laugh

The Fool

I can't get that look
out of my mind
as I was saying goodbye
when you asked me
to stay the night
your eyes were teary
and it broke my heart...

up until then
I didn't think
it mattered to you
whether I stayed
or go --
I've been so focused on
not getting hurt,
I suddenly realized
I was hurting you worse...

I don't deserve you anymore
(I was a fool)

Ruined

for the first time
in my life
I let myself hope
and dream
and it
ruined me

Over

When I stopped asking
and you stopped explaining
That's when I knew
it was over...

Revenge

imsorry imsorry imsorry imsorry imsorry
imsorry imsorry imsorry imsorry imsorry
imsorry imsorry imsorry imsorry imsorry
imsorry imsorry imsorry imsorry imsorry
imsorry imsorry imsorry imsorry imsorry....

you did it
first
you hurt me
worse

and im sorry
i've become
this person...

i used to be better --
i wanted to
love
you
forever

our love has
changed
from once
before,

and
i can't be
a doormat
anymore...

im sorry.

Between

Your fingers glide and caress beneath the
sheets...
my body gently awaking...
stroking until I whimper and writhe under
your touch,
and soon I'm shaking
your hands go faster now
as you bury your mouth upon my breasts
fingers sliding deep inside my honey
as your thumb rubs my clit
soon I'm exploding again, begging you for it
you dive your face between my legs
licking, devouring
until I shake again and again
finally I push you away
And you know
I want you deep within
please please please
you thrust so hard i gasp for air
passionately moving
through space and time
between these sheets
we share
one breath
one body

one mind
until there's nothing left
making love
has always been
what we're best
at

Gone

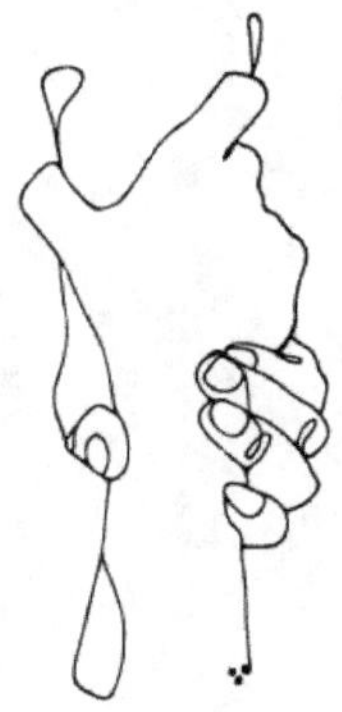

if i close my
eyes
sometimes
i can still see
the life
we were meant to have

but the more
i try
to hold
onto it
the faster
it slips
from
my mind

Triggers

I could cry a thousand times
be kissed a thousand times
make love every single night
and still have good days
but something will strike me
down to remind me of
what you did
and I'm back at the beginning
of this

Underneath

I know it's not in my head but you
got me feeling this way again -
So many questions
but never complete answers
It's underneath the surface,
I feel it -
I'm trying so hard to believe you
But what I feel won't go away
"It's in the past,
I'm different now," you say
But it's not in my head
It's been happening again
It's underneath the surface,
I feel it....

Slow Death

I don't know how
I got to this point
But everything inside
Feels like poison

Falsehoods

I'm merely an
afterthought —
You say I'm not…
Then prove it.

When We First Fell

41

Take me back to 900 days ago
When you were enamored by me
And every touch was electric

Eclipse

Your shadow
eclipses the sun —
I live in the darkness
Of your love

Avoidance

43

I could have been
Bleeding at your feet
And you would have
Just walked right
Over me…

Wasteful Wishing

She just wanted someone
with kind eyes, a tender touch
and gentle honesty
Someone that could
make her laugh,
someone without
a secret plan —
Someone that didn't use her
because they were lonely
or who didn't see her
as a trophy,
Someone
who knew that
intimacy was
about connection,
not just bodies
intersecting —
Someone who didn't
add up expenses
and keep a scoresheet
She wondered if such a
person even existed
or was she wasting time
wishing?

The Parts That Fell Away
When You Left

I have to cry
I have to write
and release these
feelings inside
I have to sleep and
remember
how to breathe
again
I have to grieve most of all;
go back and collect
the parts
that fell
away when you left —
in order
for my soul
to find its way back
to myself
so that I may finally be whole
so that I may be present
so that I may live again

Cursed

From the first time
we touched
It was the end
of all ends —
tainted, cursed…
From that point on
things only got worse
and I guess
we got
what we deserved

On The Rocks

Like a smooth charming bourbon
you make me loosen
up
My hair tumbles down
and I relax
My body opens to your
touch
It feels so good
even though
I know I know I know
it's bad for me
I want more
it's never enough
until suddenly
It's too much
and I'm sick to my stomach
and we're
fighting again

We Did This

you broke my heart
because of her —
and came back
because of him —
and now
we're slowly
killing this

The Past

Don't love me
Don't miss me
I'm just a shell
Of who
I used to be
I can't be the
person you
want me to be
Not after everything.

Irony

She hoped
that one day
he'd come back
and realize
the error of his ways
And when he did
she couldn't
forgive him

Who Am I?

I've lived
with this pain
for so long
I don't know
who I am
without it

Never Enough

She just wanted
to be the one
woman he'd choose
again and again —
In a crowded room
or across the moon
She wanted to know
she would always be his

We didn't stand a chance…

Of course you pushed me away
neither of us
knew how to be loved

Betrayal

It will always be
you three —
never you and me

Tattoo

Your name is
etched in my
heart
~~and always will be~~
I'm getting
it removed.

Realization

It's not a matter
of choosing you or him —
It's about
choosing myself

Once More

I'm here
if you want to find me
I'm here
if you want to be found
I'm where you left me
By the door
broken, half naked
on the floor
Come find me, don't keep
me waiting
Come find me,
and we can
hurt each other
once more

Downward Spiral

I can't seem to sort out my life
Why why
do I do this to myself
They say to follow your heart
but it leads to trouble
I need help,
real help
but I'm too scared to tell
I always make the worst decisions
I'm living in my own prison

You Were My Siren Song

I was so deeply, unapologetically in love with you. I poured everything I had into you, without a second thought, because being with you and making you happy was all I cared about. I couldn't see what was happening at the time but I began to change; I stopped taking care of myself. Things weren't going well and I tried harder. I put my feelings aside when you seemed upset or impatient, kept thinking things would work out eventually. I thought I was being strong but loving you made me weak; loving you meant hating me because deep down, I knew this wasn't good for me. I realize that I died too many times trying to hold on, believing we were meant to be. I should have just seen what was right in front of me. Loving you was the loneliest time of my life, and the most pitiful version of myself.

Apathy

Eventually you get to a point
where you start treating
them the way
they've been treating you
I hate to admit
even kind souls
have limits….
Why does it feel
so good to
not care anymore?
I know this can't be right
but it's better than before

Endless Cycle

My words might seem harsh
but your actions keep
breaking my heart
I love you, so I stay —
You love me, but won't change
We can't keep living
this way

It was November...

and the sun was shining so bright
I cried in your arms
you held me tight
but I still felt the pain
coursing through my veins
my bones, my womanhood
I didn't know what hurt more:
My mutilated body
Or decimated heart
Shaking and stumbling
you helped me to the car
and I continued to cry
until we got home
I couldn't look at you
I couldn't look at anything
I was no longer there
Nothing felt real except
the tears falling down my cheeks

Fate

maybe it's our fate
to love each other from afar
with all our hearts
like the sun and moon,
I'll always be
barely
within reach
of you…

The Way You Broke Me

I know it's breaking
your heart
saying you'd wait
everytime we touch
we fall in love
But I know I'll hurt you
the same way you hurt me
I wish I was good like before
I loved you more openly, gently;
but my heart has grown cold
I can't stay any longer
I'll only break your heart
the way you broke mine

Lost

Nothing is what it seems
The lines are blurred —
Up is down
right is wrong
I'm no longer
who I once was

Numbness

I can't do this anymore.
I'm sorry. I tried.
I love you.
I lied.

Never

I will never again wait
for a man
to love me,
to be with me, to put me on pause —
Now or never
all or nothing
Don't use me for satisfaction
Don't promise me the world
I'm no longer that naive girl
I've learned time and time again
love ends
and forever
is never forever.
Never.

Bleed

You're so deep inside
of my skin and bones
I would rather cut you out
and bleed
than to ever be hurt
by you again

Patterns

My questions trigger your impatience
My avoidance makes you anxious
I get mad, then sad
and you cry when we fight
you tell me not to
hold things inside
yet you
do it all the time

Here, There

Existing in the past and present
I am neither here nor there
At any given moment
I am happy and sad
And when you hold my hand
I feel your love -
But I ~~don't~~ want to run
I ~~don't~~ want to let go
I hide from the sun
And I cry alone

Please

Please don't be gentle right now
I need to hear you,
to feel your
heart pulsating
hands trembling
aching to touch me —
The hunger of your kisses
and body wishing
to taste me
Yes, sometimes
I want it slow
but please devour me
own me
control me
and don't let go

Read Me

I was a book
wanting to be read
and understood
You skimmed through it before
comprehending
what it took
to unravel the mystery
and history —
I wanted to be relished
reread
but you just wanted
to get
to the end

All Along

I've waited so long
for this
to be resolved
There doesn't seem
to be a solution -
I have to accept
my mistakes and move on
I regret
that I didn't do it sooner
the truth has been
there all along
and I've been
disillusioned

Until You Touched Me

I have always
hated my skin
my body
my hair—
Until you touched
and smelled
and licked
every part of me

Untitled

Sometimes I wish
that I just
died
the day you broke
my heart

Masochist

I knew I was bound
to get hurt
but I didn't
stop myself

(NPD)

There are many things
you will never understand
such as empathy, regret, remorse —
you are blind to
what you've done to me
and what you continue to do
You can't comprehend
anyone but yourself
That is, you are
emotionally unaware -
Lacking accountability
and ability to change

Pisces Moon

I stuck around and waited
You'd disappear for weeks,
give me scraps when you
felt the need
to keep me holding on -
I was a fool for you
I was a fool for love
I was never enough
I waited for
your texts
yet you only messaged
when wanting sex
But I stuck around
and waited —
I believed
every word you said
and sadly, still do
I was a fool for you
I was a fool for love
I was never enough
A love like ours
is never saved
even if we try
and behave —
we are giving each

other an early grave…
You'd disappear for days
then say: I love you baby
gave scraps when you felt
the need to keep me
holding on
I stuck around and waited
(still waiting)
You said you're no longer lying
(still lying)
and I'm still
slowly dying
each day —
I am a fool for you
I am a fool for love
I will never be enough

What You Get

It's hard to smile or laugh
It's hard to pretend I'm not sad
Don't be mad that I'm not the same
You're the one who took your love away
I will never ever look at you
with the same eyes
or gaze upon your face
I would have died for you
Now all I do is cry over you
Doesn't matter if you're sorry
Doesn't matter if you regret it
You shattered every lovable,
eager, naive piece of me —
So this is the version you get.

One Step at a Time

There's too much suffering
in a lifetime
I've lost my passion for living —
I tell myself,
just put one foot
in front of the other
and it's more than
I can bear.
The reason I keep
walking is the hope
of being found
by the one who is
meant to love me…
And then I can finally
fall into his arms,
exhausted, from such a long journey —
and he will say,
"You're safe now,
rest easy,
I will love you faithfully
until eternity."
And I will sigh,
relieved.

Self-Loathing

She doesn't need you
to bring her down —
after all she's been through,
she could destroy you -
easily,
seamlessly;
But she prefers
to destroy herself.

Trying

I guess unloving you
is really just learning how
to love myself —
Because after all you've
done to me,
what else could it mean?
The only way I'll ever recover
and finally be free
is to tell the
little girl inside:
you deserve better
we deserve better…

Self Deception

I keep asking you for the truth
because I've caught you
but I realize
that I've been lying too —
I've been lying to myself
that things will change
and we'll eventually be okay

Years Ago

There was a young couple sitting on a bench: they were both in tears, her arms wrapped around him. I immediately recognized it - the fear of being torn apart, unable to share a life together; clinging to whatever moments you have. Maybe it was forbidden love or the timing wasn't right.

I was them once, years ago. The pain of not knowing when I'd see him again, wondering if this was the end… terrified of letting go, wanting the minutes to last forever. It was all too real - my heart broke for them.

Compassion

She noted the look of despair on my face
and asked if I knew—
I said I didn't…
He lied, she said
I started to panic - I'm so sorry
She looked at me with compassion and told
me about her own
devastating relationship
in less than 30 seconds
My eyes welled up and I was so
unbelievably grateful to be seen
and understood "You're going to be okay."
And just those simple words from a
stranger,
a beautiful kind stranger,
made me feel a little bit of hope.

That's the power of women helping women.
Men break us —
but our sisters
lift us up in a way no one
else does…
and help us put the pieces back together.

The Quiet Truth

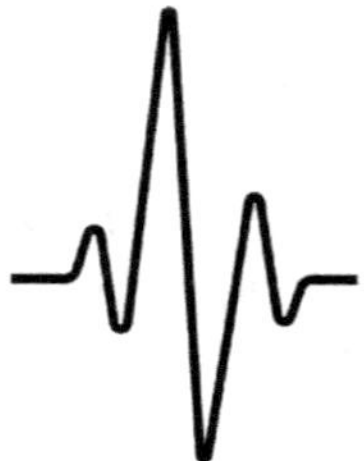

I stormed out into the cold air
chasing down the moon, going as fast as I
possibly could
I needed to run, to gulp air until my lungs
exploded
and legs fell off — until all I would feel
is pain coursing through every cell,
until I was left with raw pure agony…
Everything that happened, all the anguish
I've fought to keep at bay was
forcing its way through, I could feel it
seeping, threatening to consume me
and I was terrified to let this darkness inside
take hold of me
I collapsed in the grass, face buried in the
ground

wishing that I was covered deep deep deep
underneath it all.
Tears were pouring from my eyes but I
barely felt them -
each moment was just a debilitating
breath after another…
I struggled to move
*I'm so tired… tired of it all. When will it end?
There's no point to this. I can't do it
anymore.*

Silence. The darkness was quiet.
Minutes passed.
My breathing was slower but I was still
aching everywhere. I decided I wasn't
going to get up, I would lay there
indefinitely.
But there was a voice —
a voice that I heard through my heart, not
my ears and it said:

You've been through a lot
abuse, abandonment, assault, betrayal,
loss, excruciating nerve pain,
you were told you might never walk again
and fought for two years to literally get back
on your feet…
you've battled depression, anxiety, infidelity,
financial hardship, loneliness…

what if you just get up one more time? what
if your story deserves a better ending?

I lay there contemplating. There was no
such thing as a better ending. Just an
ending.
*No, leave me alone. I just want to sleep…
I'm so tired. Let me sleep now.*
The voice was silent.
A breeze started to blow through my hair
but I didn't move. The night grew colder, my
limbs were getting stiff. I knew if I stayed
any longer I could freeze to death.
Get up. You've slept enough, the voice said.
*I have nothing, no hope, no future, no
reason. Leave me alone.*
And your children? the voice said.
My body was screaming, bones were
vibrating
Sobs wracked through my chest as I
struggled to get up

There were no more words.

Because I remembered why I continued to
overcome

They needed me…

They have never hurt or betrayed me the
way other people have in my life
There was no choice.
There never was.
I got up.

www.ingramcontent.com/pod-product-compliance
Lightning Source LLC
LaVergne TN
LVHW011037200726
843509LV00011B/1296